WomensWords
WOMEN'S WISE WORDS

Edited by

Heather Killingray

First published in Great Britain in 2003 by
WOMENSWORDS
Remus House, Coltsfoot Drive,
Peterborough, PE2 9JX
Telephone (01733) 898101
Fax (01733) 313524

All Rights Reserved

Copyright Contributors 2003

SB ISBN 1 84418 253 3

FOREWORD

Although we are a nation of poetry writers we are accused of not reading poetry and not buying poetry books: after many years of listening to the incessant gripes of poetry publishers, I can only assume that the books they publish, in general, are books that most people do not want to read.

Poetry should not be obscure, introverted, and as cryptic as a crossword puzzle: it is the poet's duty to reach out and embrace the world.

The world owes the poet nothing and we should not be expected to dig and delve into a rambling discourse searching for some inner meaning.

The reason we write poetry (and almost all of us do) is because we want to communicate: an ideal; an idea; or a specific feeling. Poetry is as essential in communication, as a letter; a radio; a telephone, and the main criteria for selecting the poems in this anthology is very simple: they communicate.

CONTENTS

Equal Rights	Doris Black	1
Fire-Food	Jill Berntsson	2
I Heard Her Call Me From Far Away	Carolyn Atkinson	3
Why Are We Here?	Avril McKerhie	4
Modern Woman	Sonia Ruckley	6
Digging For Treasure	Carol Reid	7
Time	Teresa Prout	8
Now That I Am Old	Isobel Swade	10
Let Your Kiss Be My Guide	Michelle Stock	11
Living Alone	Jill Lowe	12
Life's Betrayal	Ann Hailey	13
Elhanan Hillel	Zena Zulman	14
A Man's World	Alison J Smith	15
The Unborn Child	May Frazer	16
The Breadwinner	Kerry Scott-Gillett	17
The Farmer's Wife	Janet Llewellyn	18
My Life An Ocean	Lynn Beesley	19
Untitled	Christine Clare	20
Shape Of His Heart	Kate Denyer	21
Bouncing Back	Paula Wilde	22
Untitled	Rosina Forward	23
Please Mum	Elaine Nicol	24
Alone	Rachel Clissold	25
Who Am I?	Vida Taylor	26
Own Child	Emma Verity	27
Before You Know It	Avril Cowan	28
Here's Hoping	E Smith	29
Meadowsweet	Pam O'Connor	30
Middle-Aged Women	Hazel Maddox	31
Untitled	Rita Parchment	32
Little Miracle	Eileen Swift	33
Lonely Wife	Julie Heath	34
Betrayed	Lynsey Carroll	35
Equality	Pearlina Lindsay	36
Untitled	Hilary Southam	37

A Woman In 2003	Mira Love	38
Marriage	Margaret Dunn	39
Heartbroken	Cindy James	40
My Delights	Dorothy Slater	42
Heartbreak	Helen Ford	43
Life's Gifts	Lola Perks-Hartnell	44
Stephen Our Son	Hazel Millard	45
The Truth?	Catherine Fitzpatrick	46
Women In Motion	Amy Shelton Goodall	47
21st Century Woman	Audrey J Henton	48
Men Versus Women	Susan Ellis	49
Midlife Choice	J Ramsden	50
Why?	Cynthia Glasby	51
Only Joking . . . Or Am I?	Colly	52
Solitude	Chris Hill	53
Age 50	Linda J Ventura	54
If Only	Elizabeth Hayden-Jones	55
What Women Do For Love	Rita Melia	56
The Invisible Me	Pauline Bowden	57
I Want To Be A Perfect Mum	Hilary Higton	58
Stop	Michaela Jayne Fairley	60
Who's She?	Dizzy D	61
You Are Not Alone	Pamela Carder	62
Help Me!	Ema Charnock	63
Feeling This Way	Amanda Hopley	64
Him!	Jackie Sutton	65
Cheating	Joan E Blissett	66
Trapped	Cari Hilaire	67
Justice	Joyce M Jones	68
Who's For Justice?	Margaret Gurney	69
What Price The Sisterhood?	Jan Yule	70
The Demon Drink	Kim Montia	71
Poem Regarding Being A Woman	H A Speight	72
A Job Please	Valerie Smallwood	73
Housewife Blues	D Mason	74
If Only . . .	Penny Pritchard	76
Dementia	Stella Copson	77

A Woman's World	Margaret McGowan	78
To An Absent Friend	Mary Hughes	79
Her Eyes Don't Sparkle Anymore	Ann Hathaway	80
Moving Home	Kathleen Elaine Evans	81
To Me	Mary Tickle	82
What Is Love . . . ?	June Melbourn	83
What You See	M M Graham	84
To Forgive	Elizabeth Leach	85
Woman's Work	Gail Sturgess	86
A Woman's World	Jean P McGovern	87
Somebody's Sweetheart	Hilary J Cairns	88
The Snow-Capped Hill	Joan Magennis	89
Down To The Shelter	Doris Kirby	90
A Tale Of Two Dogs	Rosemary Davies	92
Forgiving	Pearl M Burdock	93
Far Away	Sophie Long	94
Judge Me Not	Donna-Marie Capper	95
I Still Love You	Shahdaroba	96
The Wedding Day	Pamela Matthews	97
Love Will Come	Paula M R Jackson	98
A Single Flower	John Terry	99
To Be Alone	S Stark	100
Broken Heart	Joyce Sherwood	101
Forbidden Love	Jennifer Jackson	102
Reflecting On The Past	Susan Turner	103
My Love's Cherished Memory	Christine Cyster	104
The Path Of Love	Ise Obomhense	105
Love's Pit	Pamela Preston	106
New Valentine	K Townsley	107
Not Alone	Morag Kilpatrick	108
Dear Jack	Joan Fletcher	109
As Times Go By	Carrie Stuart	110
Losing You	Diane Stead	111
Missing You	J Preston	112
Soul Journey	Marian Jones	113
Forever	Emma Scott	114

EQUAL RIGHTS

Equal rights. What equal rights?
Did we really have a lot to gain?
For however much we have succeeded
Men still don't get the birthing pain.

Doris Black

Fire-Food

Do not value my endeavour,
not now, not soon, not ever!
Instead ponder on
the dusty surface that's not gone,
because I dared to stop and write,
and carried on into the night.

I'm only worth a pile of clothes,
neatly ironed, shirts in rows.
All else that I would choose to do,
mere fire-food to the likes of you.
When my soul is in the nude,
you perceive a lazy mood.
My feelings are inconsequential,
the household humming, now that's essential!

Jill Berntsson

I Heard Her Call Me From Far Away

I heard her call her from far away.
Deep in the ground where my ancestors lay.
Help me my mother, take the tears that I weep,
Wrap me in your blanket and rock me to sleep.

Show me the woodlands that call me by name,
Give me the love that takes away pain.
The stress you removed and showed me sunrise
No rain anymore or thunderous skies.

I need you to show me what life's really about,
Give me understanding and take away doubt,

Freedom, I crave for, oh Mum take me home,
Back to the land where my ancestors roam.
Love me and feed me but never despair,
Give me back life that comes from your heart.

Carolyn Atkinson

WHY ARE WE HERE?

Some relationships last
And some have to be put in the past
Why on earth do we have so much emotion
When other people have no devotion?

Are we loved, are we adored
Or are we there to stop men being bored?
If we are married, or if we are single
We are female, we get out and mingle.

You can be a good cook
Who needs a recipe book
Life can be good and life can be bad
We are women and of that we are glad.

Do we really want a man to be there
When all you do is argue and swear?
We want someone who loves us and treats us good
Who doesn't go in a huff and goes in a mood.

When we meet the one we love
Do we see a white dove?
We want to be with someone that's a lover and a friend
Someone to be with you until life's end.

Then we hear the word baby
You don't know, you're thinking maybe,
You give up your job and single life
To stay at home to be mum and wife.

Is your man a happy chappie
If he has to stay home and change a nappy?
Your life now you have to change
For next 16 years you rearrange.

Men you can't live with them
You can't live without them.
We know when you find one that's special from the start
He will always have a place in your heart.

Avril McKerhie

MODERN WOMAN

Can't knit anymore
Although they don't have to.
Can't mend anymore
Don't need to, that's true.

Women can't bake now
Can't bare to be at home.
'What you think we are?'
Is their indignant moan.

When they do marry
Having had sex for years,
Insist on wearing white,
The shallow little dears.

Mostly they get the house
And kids, when they split,
Then in they bring a stranger
They just don't care a s**t!

People say that they go
Clubbing and get canned.
I'm not sure what it means
Often some have one night stands.

Always wearing trousers
Like men they want to be,
Unlike the Mona Lisa
They'll lose their mystery.

But I'm a lady,
Old now, my time has gone,
Nevertheless I still think,
The way they act, *is wrong!*

Sonia Ruckley

DIGGING FOR TREASURE

We're digging for treasure, my daughters and me,
The wind makes our ears ring, but we're happy.

There's no gold horizon; no aqua blue sea,
Just gritty wet sand and my daughters and me.

Pebbles so many and shells ten-a-penny and
Feathers that once covered magical wings.

We're digging for treasure; and wonder and pleasure
Is giving us reason to search, we three,
By the side of this grey, northern sea.

We're digging for treasure, my daughters and me,
Their small world rotating, for now, around me.

So small either side, with eyes full of wonder -
I'm wishing this moment could last a bit longer.

Inquisitive faces and outstretched arms
Triumphantly grasping in tiny palms
Their pebbles and feathers and shells ten-a-penny
That over the years have been grasped by many.

Don't be too sad girls if no treasure's found.
I see you, and I know it's all above ground.

Carol Reid

Time

Rushing here,
Dashing there,
Have I time to brush my hair?

Mouths to feed,
Garden to weed,
Having to fulfil family's needs,

Washing here,
Ironing there,
Oh, for five minutes in a chair,

Shopping again,
Here comes the rain,
Forgot the shopping list, oh what a pain,

Vacuuming's boring,
Husband's snoring,
Oh-oh, phone bill final warning,

Brushing the dog,
Walking the cat,
Oh, which way round was that?

End of the day,
Time to lay,
My weary bones down in the hay,

Dreams so deep,
Oh, what's that bleep?
Time to get up? But I've just gone to sleep!

Nothing to wear,
Greying hair,
Bosses that don't really seem to care,

It's Friday at last and I'm so glad,
I think I was going slightly mad,
The weekend - hooray! More fun to be had!

Teresa Prout

NOW THAT I AM OLD

Now that I am old, I may colour my hair bright green,
No one would notice, the old are seldom seen.
Now that I am old, I can say what I like, think my own thoughts
Even ride a bike wearing bright red shorts.
Now that I am old, I care less what people say
I want to live every day as if it's my last
Who knows - it may be, life goes so fast.
Now that I am old, I intend to have more fun
Act as though my life has just begun.
Being old is not so bad - the alternative is rather sad.
So cheer up all who approach this time
Remember me and read this rhyme.

Isobel Swade

LET YOUR KISS BE MY GUIDE

Hold me close, don't let go,
Guide your fingertips, take it slow.
Pull me near, make me belong,
Tightly, keep me strong.
Run your fingers through my hair,
And upon my eyes feast your stare.
Hold me close, don't let go,
Whisper the words I need to know.

Guide my touch, to make it right,
Hold me in your arms tonight.
Keep the wind out of my face,
Lift me to that faraway place.
Show me heaven, in your eyes,
Lift me up and touch the skies.
You and I will reach the stars,
As you hold me close, inside your arms.

We'll slowly glide on past the moon,
The ending so far, but will arrive so soon.
Head spinning on a high of pleasure,
I'll keep this night with me forever.
Hold me close, and hold me tight,
Say I'm the one for you tonight.
And then tell me that it's meant to be,
You and I, for eternity.

Hold me close, don't let go,
Whisper the words I need to know.
Run your fingers along my face,
My lips with yours, do trace.
The warmth from your body next to mine,
Sets fires alight in my eyes.
Hold me closely, let us belong,
Together, eternally as one.

Michelle Stock

LIVING ALONE

I love the peace and quiet,
I never feel lonely, I never feel blue.
I can always find things, I like to do,
It's a life full of freedom,
No one depends on me,
I'm not responsible if someone is sad.
I don't have to listen, to them going mad,
No one to shout and swear or slam the doors.
Ask me, 'What's for tea?'
Do the household chores.
When I get home from work at night
And home is silent, there's no one there,
I don't think lonely, I think bliss,
I haven't got a care,
Cook my tea, settle down for the night
And watch TV,
Summer evenings are just great.
The nights are light, the air is warm,
Shall I do some gardening,
Shall I mow the lawn,
Shall I cook or just sit and read a good book,
Shall I wash my hair,
Choose the clothes I wear,
Go out with friends,
Have a dance and a laugh,
Freedom and peace are what I like best,
No need to go searching
For happiness.

Jill Lowe

LIFE'S BETRAYAL

True love, life's misfortunes leave their deep mark.
Eyes meet, paths cross, enchanted lovers date.
With sorrowful heart, moonset, into the dark.

Hearts entwine, growing closer, hear them hark.
Love grows, marriage calls, become my soul mate.
True love, life's misfortunes leave their deep mark.

With child and more, love still new you can lark.
Home you make, with garden and golden gate.
With sorrowful heart, moonset, into the dark.

Nightmares now, it's not a walk, in the park.
My love goes astray, informs my fate.
True love, life's misfortunes leave their deep mark.

My emotions stripped away like bark.
Love grows to anger, betrayal and hate.
With sorrowful heart, moonset, into the dark.

You've left my empty heart, cold and stark.
You want forgiveness, but, it's far too late.
True love, life's misfortunes leave their mark.
With sorrowful heart, moonset, into the dark.

Ann Hailey

ELHANAN HILLEL
(For her husband on their 19th wedding anniversary)

Elhanan Hillel
I fell under your spell
My life is so sublime
Since the day that you were mine
In friendship and in love
Like spirits from above
You are my life's desire
You set my heart on fire

There is no other one
Under the moon or sun
Who is a saint like you
These words of mine are true

There is no other man for me
In your arms I am still free
I miss you when you are near
Your absence I fear.

Zena Zulman

A MAN'S WORLD

Can somebody tell me, the meaning of life?
So I won't end up as some old geezer's wife.

Can somebody tell me, the meaning of hope?
So in this strange world, I might learn to cope.

But nobody can, I've asked everyone,
And they all say the same, 'Nothing can be done.'

But I won't take that answer - the world will have to change.
Because I will never, be locked in that cage.

That traps so many people, in this thing called normality,
I will never . . . surrender my sanity.

I know these are big words, from someone as young as me,
But I will not get stuck, I will continue being free.

There has to be something better, I can do with my life,
Than just ending up, as some old geezer's wife!

Alison J Smith

THE UNBORN CHILD

This place is dark and safe and warm
I fear no ill while I am here
But what awaits I cannot know
I wish for peace and loved ones near.

My mother's heart beats soft and strong
The sound of it lulls me to sleep.
She speaks to me in tones of love
I pray I never make her weep.

She awaits my birth with fear and joy
Will I fulfil her deepest needs?
I know I'll be her precious child
As each successive year proceeds.

May Frazer

THE BREADWINNER

Precious child, do you know
Where your sweet Mummy goes,
When she hugs you goodbye,
Softly kisses your nose?
Abandons you sobbing
At the nursery door,
Tries to ignore your tears
As they roll to the floor.

Filled with sadness and guilt
She drives slowly away,
To face yet another
Tedious working day.
Wishing she had the choice
To stay at home with you,
But with bills to be paid,
Earning money wins through.

Kerry Scott-Gillett

The Farmer's Wife

Once you were young and strong,
and I, so innocent, did wait and long
for love unbounded, to match the burning
of my troubled heart.
Each day I waited, hoping that your warmth
would be transferred to me,
our lives entwined - not torn apart.

All day I worked beside you on the land,
my body bent, unfeeling to the pain.
Outside we were together, but not one,
and yet I felt your need. We tilled, we sowed,
- each crop a symbol standing proud and tall,
the off-spring of our hands; but that was all.

If only you had loved me as our sons,
those strong, straight men, who followed at your will.
They grew in strength, while I dried up with age,
wilting, like blossoms in the noonday sun.
And now too late, I watch you too grow old,
no sap, just withered roots; your blood still cold.

Janet Llewellyn

MY LIFE AN OCEAN

With your emerald green hue
and dashing white swell
life on earth can be just hell
we ebb along forever it seems
together we strive in the battle of life
you are the mother, I am the wife
we're strong and brave, we will win through
to thyself we will be true
as I wade into your loving embrace
your arms hold me tight
you fill me with wonder and awe
we share the gift to make new life
I shall die but you will go on
as we part our tears will cascade
now we must part like waves in a storm
with the squalls and the calms we will get by
at least I have given it a try.

Lynn Beesley

Untitled

A woman's role as a mother,
Is a job, that's never done.
From the moment your kids can
Master the word.
All you can ever hear is . . . 'Mum'!
Like me, in my situation.
While bringing up my five,
They'd all shout 'Mum' in fine chorus!
My head was always alive!
I'd wake up in a morning
My time was never my own.
Mum do this, have you got that,
Not giving me space for a moan!
A way of life, and I liked it,
Wouldn't dream of it
Any other way.
It's all I ever got used to
Hearing, 'Mum', in my ears
Night and day!
No time to myself to be pampered
To dream of some far away place
I tried, oh I tried to sit quiet
But, they'd always end up
In my face!

Christine Clare

SHAPE OF HIS HEART

When all it does is seem to go wrong
A feeling meant to last but causes heartbreak for so long
All it does is put you down
Sinking so deep you begin to drown
Causes so much pain, leaves you bleeding on the ground
A feeling never lost, a feeling always found
Falling deeper into emotion, deeper into thought
Always a pleasure with which you fought
If it was meant to be, why did it cause so much hurt
Thrown away and collected as if you were dirt
Unable to breath, be who you really are
No longer yourself, that special star
Not wanting to let him down, forever trying to impress
Every time you tried, you just got less
He could leave you stranded, make you all alone
But would come running back for the love you'd shown
He could give you the end without the fresh start
But that would not be the shape of his heart.

Kate Denyer

BOUNCING BACK

My one and only, forever we say
Not knowing what life will bring our way
We betroth ourselves all innocent and sweet
Thinking in our hearts no one else like him we'll meet

But time takes its toll and something goes wrong
It hurts when you hear the tune that was 'our song'
Love has died so sad, never thought this would be me
Friends promise a future that's brighter - just you see!

And so we oblige and go for just one drink
Hoping no further into this misery we sink
It's horrid being my age and single once more
Oh gosh they feel sorry for me - I'm such a bore!

But hey I'm not dead and the laughter creeps in
And I learn that to enjoy myself isn't a sin
So I enjoy where I am and the love that abounds
And my family and friends look smugly around

OK I say I've learned how to be *me!*
Not 'his' or 'theirs' and I am just happy to be
So when you are feeling sad and there's nowhere to go
Remember you are a person and special - believe me I know.

Paula Wilde

UNTITLED

Nigel dear your talents are wasted here.
Banking is not your profession.
With pen and paper in your hand
You could teach us all a lesson.
Like the late Dillwyn Thomas
Whose poems made him famous
Poor soul, not until he was dead and gone
So Nigel please carry on
And knowing one day, that we will all say
Nigel's name will go down great in history.
In the breathless hush of the evening
And the quiet and still of the night
There is one Rosina Forward that wants
Nigel to write and write and write.

Rosina Forward

PLEASE MUM

My mum, she doesn't speak to me,
We fell out long ago,
Oh how I wish she'd call me,
To say, 'I miss you so'.

We were more than mother and daughter,
Sharing long days full of laughter,
Then it all came to an end,
When I lost my bestest friend.

Through no fault of hers or mine,
The light's gone out, no longer shines,
We pass each other in the street,
Each too stubborn to be beat.

When I was a little lass,
She never had to make a pass,
To swipe at me for something done,
I was just too full of fun.

I wish things could be as they were,
Back to friends who really care,
She never said, 'I told you so',
Even when I was so low.

Right now I wish we'd speak again,
Go shopping and be friends again,
To speak to her not as my mum,
I don't want all, I just want some.

Elaine Nicol

ALONE

I'm here all alone in my room,
With just a small light on,
If it weren't for you, I wouldn't be writing these lyrics,
And this light would be gone.

I'd still be here alone,
But I'd be in complete darkness,
Knowing nothing can hurt me,
And everything is harmless.

I try to think what I can do,
But all I think about is you
I try to keep you out my head, but you're appearing in my dreams,
Broken ice is where I tread,
Well that's how it seems.

To make this life complete
I've got to fight for every dream
And not be in defeat
Not live life on a beam

I don't think you understand
There's so much I need to say to you
So just take my hand
And do the things you're able to do

You gave me the strength I need to be here
You showed me it was real
Made me have no fear
Give me time to heal.

Rachel Clissold (16)

WHO AM I?

A face among the millions,
Fairly blank and fairly plain,
What is it that I'm doing here?
A face without a name.

Once I knew I was someone,
I knew me very well,
But along the years I lost myself,
To a face without a name.

I wonder is it only me,
Who values such a gift,
The gift that is identity,
A face that needs a name.

One day I'll search to find myself,
And know just who I'll be,
Not the person others want,
This face belongs to me.

Vida Taylor

Own Child

Happiness lies in the arms of life
Sweet breath of innocence.
Rose petal softness brushes your mouth,
Sweet breath of innocence.

Thistledown is your hair
Violet are your eyes
The dappling of sunlight
In the dimples of your smile.

Laughter ripples through my soul
Sweet breath of innocence
Eyes sore with sorrow, wide with delight
Sweet breath of innocence.

Emma Verity

BEFORE YOU KNOW IT

Before you know it . . .
That opportunity
To lend a hand
To give a hug
To say a thanks
It passes by . . .
And why, oh, why
Did I not take that chance
To show I care,
To turn a glare
Into a smile?
Don't hesitate, or speculate . . .
Life is too short

Before you know it
It's too late . . .
So do not wait
To make that move
Give out your love
Be first to show it
Before you know it
It's too late . . .

Avril Cowan

HERE'S HOPING

Did the vote for women really bring equality as such?
Or are we still struggling to prove we know as much?
As much as men I really mean, can we possible compare?
To prove we have the knowledge, let's face it do they care?

To strive for equal rights seems unequal to say the least
They laugh when girls struggle as if their education has deceased.
Women can pilot planes, are astronauts, they can also show they care
Do we question what the men do? Let's face it would we dare?

Let's see men holding down a job, childcare, housework,
                                looking after partner too
As well as doing the garden, school run and being a loving partner true.
So we have to keep on trying to prove we are as good as any men
Tell them we are as good as them time and time again!

E Smith

MEADOWSWEET

Look out the window at spring
Proud green shoots on everything that appeared lifeless

Life is like the annual seasons
Sunny and cloudy moods defying all reason

Midway through life another cycle begins
Bringing the warmth and tenderness of another spring

Time cannot deny winter's destruction
The cold and misery on nature's instruction

But it teaches us a new compassion
And the discovery that our life is on ration

Personal ambition seems to matter less
It's the love of a friend we need to caress

Here is the sunshine of our being
The warmth in our hearts giving our life meaning

The sharing of time, closeness of thought
Is the soul's music tenderly taught

When such affection has been born
It should be shared not denied or suffer scorn

For nature has shown her kindest face
When putting friendships in their place

Like a field of meadowsweet her queenly remark
Bringing joy before winter's dark.

Pam O'Connor

MIDDLE-AGED WOMEN

I look in the mirror
And what do I see?
I swear it's my mother
Looking at me!

The lines and the shadows,
They weren't there before
They 'snook up' and hit me
Of that I am sure.

The thread veins and hard skin
Both seem to abound,
And *I know* that my bum
Was never that round!

Is it just me who thinks it?
I'm not really sure.
But I hope that they find
A really good cure!

Why do I care
Some people may say?
But when gravity hits you
It won't go away!

I spend time in the bathroom,
Putting things right.
I get up so early
It's almost still night!

What can I do,
To combat my plight?
Why - take out my contacts
I improve with short sight!

Hazel Maddox

UNTITLED

There is a God above up high,
watching down from the sky, or an angel close by,
that can no longer see you pray and cry,
for hope to end the endless pain,
of the sick and dying of those most dear,
to worldwide crimes, to a bloody war, a suicide,
someone on the edge who can't take no more,
a homeless man, unwanted child, the list goes on.
But as His life we all do share, at one time or another,
a broken heart and tears that flow,
and comfort from one another.

Rita Parchment

LITTLE MIRACLE

When I look down at that cute little face
That cute little smile
That makes my heart race
I still can't believe that you are here
After waiting so long, year after year.
You look so tiny lying there
Kicking little feet, waving hands in the air
My prayers were answered
When God sent this little angel
In my arms he did place
What name should I give you,
Surely it must be . . . Grace.

Eileen Swift

Lonely Wife

As I sit here all alone
Watching tele and answering the phone
The kids in bed, lay fast asleep.
While I sit down and rest my feet
The husband's out, I don't know where
But for these few hours I don't care
He'll be back full of ale
Laying down the law adding to my pain
He will not stop until he's asleep
He'll wake next morning being so sweet
Not a thought of what went on
Just as long as I tag along.

Julie Heath

BETRAYED

I was just a small child when he betrayed my trust,
took my innocence, my childhood for his own sick lust,
my mind blocked it out for many, many years,
but when it resurfaced it had rage and tears,
the pain was too much I didn't want to go on,
my parents' silence, so hurtful, so wrong,
I went off the rails getting drunk and high,
one night stands, craving love, wanting to die,
then I found my soulmate, his love is so true,
I learnt how to trust and love him back too,
I'm so thankful to him for the way that he loves me,
he has helped me forgive and reach for my destiny,
the hurt's still there though, thoughts deep in my mind,
it'll always be there but I'm starting to find,
bearing hate and grudges will make sure he wins,
forgiveness and dreams stop me being his victim.

Lynsey Carroll

EQUALITY

Equality cannot be one alone,
Strength to do it, starts at home,
To gain equality, let self be the guide
From man's oppression we cannot hide.

Fists at home, guns on the streets,
Stand up sister, or face defeat
Relationship is ruined by power and oppression
Let not man continue with this obsession.

A change in attitude about man's violence
Don't lay down and suffer in silence,
Respect, the word to hold so dear
Respect ain't man with gun or fear.

Black women, Asian women, white women too
Respect yourself sister, you know this be true
The fight for equality starts with you
And grows when one becomes two.

So come on sister, speak with one voice
Inside and outside ain't no choice
Teach your children of love and equality
Let's work together for the sake of humanity.

Pearlina Lindsay

UNTITLED

You'll never keep that man my gran would say
Remembering what it was like in the good old days
You're never there when he comes home from work
And the domestic duties you always shirk.

You certainly aren't a bit like me
I always stirred your grampy's tea
Heated the water in time for his wash
Then went through his pockets looking for dosh

But things have changed I would reply
And women no longer on men rely
We are partners now with equal rights
But I do go through his pockets late at night.

But Gran would say you don't know you're born
And on my takeaway food she would scorn
Fancy not cooking a Sunday lunch
And what's this thing people coming for brunch

I can't imagine having all my chores met
Nor spending an hour scrubbing my step
Making home-made jam and fresh cooked bread
I'd much rather Tesco's and Indian instead

But my gran's sense of humour was second to none
And over the years we had lots of fun
She never understood my way of life
And I'd never experienced her trouble and strife

Now no longer with us I can only reflect
On my gran's views on life and especially sex
You don't talk about except on your own
And once you get married you must never roam.

Hilary Southam

A Woman In 2003

As a woman in two thousand and three
I'm free
not like I used to be

I was a woman owned by a man
now I do what I want because I can

I watched older generations, Mum, Gran towing the line
so I decided to be tall and straighten my spine
now I walk tall
and am having 'a ball'

I am as free as a bird
and happy when I make lemon curd

I enjoy my walks
and my talks
sharing with other women who enjoy their time
and can sit, be and make up a rhyme

Life is worth living
and I am happy giving
and sharing my experiences of life
no longer a woman of toil and strife

Gone are the days
of 'honour and obeys'

I can follow my own career
and not become a premature 'old dear'.

Mira Love

MARRIAGE

Marriage is a contract, a clever little plan,
I wonder who first thought it up
I bet it was a man.
Because it seems that on the whole, the female is misled,
To thinking that the married state, will be a rosy bed.

A woman's work it seems to me, is never really through,
No matter how much work she does,
There's always more to do,
Wash and iron, scrub the floor, change the baby, answer the door.
Shopping, cooking, making beds, all this is hers when once she weds.

Of course if this becomes a bore,
A part-time job from ten to four, might help to even up the score.
Alas, the house must still be neat and just forget those aching feet.
The evening meal must be on time,
To serve it late would be a crime.

Then whilst the family take their ease,
Replenished with hot cups of teas;
She can do the washing up and if she's lucky snatch a cup.
And later sit before the box,
To mend a pile of holey socks.

When at last it's time for bed, won't dare complain about her head.
Because it's thought of as a ruse,
A worn out line, a woman's excuse.
She must postpone the dream she had planned
And first lie back and think of England!

Margaret Dunn

HEARTBROKEN

Standing here all alone
Feeling very blue
Watching others dancing
Still thinking about you.

Thinking of our first date
It turned out sheer bliss
And even under the mistletoe
Where we shared our first kiss.

The trips we had to the beach
And paddling in the sea
The deep red rose, you had sent
With love from you to me.

Valentines and birthdays
And Christmastimes too
All of which we shared our love
All the year through.

Then one day you came to say
I've found another love
All my dreams were shattered into
Like a storm from above.

I felt so hurt deep inside
And cried myself to sleep
You said I was the only one,
You'd ever want to keep.

I will never find another love
That will ever take your place
Those sparkling eyes, your tender smile
Upon your handsome face.

Still standing here all alone
Still feeling very blue
Still watching others dancing
Still thinking about you.

The night is over, time to go
Loving couples leave the floor
I take a walk home by myself
I won't see you anymore.

Someone else has taken my place
Please try and remember me
I'm the one you left behind
Because I'll always be here, free.

Cindy James

My Delights

Sari silks on slender forms
Sunset on an isle
Virgin brides and icicles
Sweetness in a smile.

April belles and freesia smells
Gardens in a room
Big blue eyes and purple skies
Silence of the moon.

Fragrance from a granny tree
Velvet in a cheek
Baby fuzz and eider curls
Digits in a creek.

Fairy wings and silky things
Magnolia scented air
Teardrops when they're happy ones
Sunbeams on a chair.

Ribbon sheen and boughs of green
Vapour on a rose
Satin shoes and sugar floss
Diamonds in a nose.

A mass array of swan ballet
Magnificent they flow
Like bobbing blossoms on the wind
A river, say, of snow.

Dorothy Slater

HEARTBREAK

Another night of restlessness,
My life forsaken, and heart torn,
My whole world seems in such mess,
I cry to greet the coming dawn.

Why must my love be unrequited,
Why cannot me and my lover be united,
Was I betrayed there with a kiss,
And as my soul aimed, the target missed.

How often I have been here before,
Crying with the dreams that break,
My heart and soul lie bled and raw,
And from my last resource I take,
The dregs of hope within my cup,
The loving thoughts that still remain,
The faith that I must surely sup,
And with one last fling, the resource drains.

I lie again and feel the wind,
Wondering will fate or God be kind,
And ask the angels to find a form,
That they may touch me, and be warm.
So hard this life, not much more can I take,
For I surely will die of this heartbreak.

Helen Ford

LIFE'S GIFTS

We each have different gifts
To offer back to life,
Which may provide the lifts
To help a soul in strife.

A listener we may be
When someone needs an ear.
It's plain for all to see
These benefits are clear.

The gift of time to call
On someone all alone,
Who could have had a fall
And no one would have known!

And what's the good of laughter
If it's not being spread about?
It can bring joy hours after
Reflecting on fun, no doubt.

Some have gifts of art
Concrete or abstract;
There's acting for a start,
And singing, that's a fact.

Even without good health
We all have gifts to share,
Even without much wealth,
We've gifts beyond compare.

These gifts are all equal
No matter what the cost,
Here follows the natural sequel -
'Life's gifts are never lost!'

Lola Perks-Hartnell

STEPHEN OUR SON

It seems like only yesterday,
When you came into our world,
What the future held for you was yet to be unfurled.
You were a lovely, happy boy,
You gave my mom and dad such joy.

Remember Grandad made you a car of sorts,
Driving us on imaginary trip to every resorts
With a real steering wheel and a box for a seat,
Couldn't get you home for something to eat.

Can you remember you helped to build my kite,
We failed yet again as it would not take flight.

School days for you seemed a bit of a pest,
But woodwork and art brought out your best.

Then to work on the fair you wanted to go,
At first my reaction was to say no.
We went to see Tim, a man on the fair,
He put out minds at rest, as he would take care,
We missed you so, and I got so upset
When I heard your favourite Boney M on my cassette,
Before you went away you were just a lad,
But when you came back you came back a man.

Work time came along, you settled with Len,
You earned your own wages, became independent then.
Along came your first car, you had off your dad,
The freedom it gave you, how it made you feel glad.

Now you have reached 40, a maturable age,
You have settled down with Julie and your dog Blade,
So look after yourself and don't over do it,
We love you to bits, but don't always show it.

Hazel Millard

THE TRUTH?

Nothing will ever be the same again
Grief like a thief - beyond belief
His love, his talent and his care not in the frame
They scandalised his name
Nothing will ever be the same again

That betrayal of his name portrayed him as a loser
Negated his sobriety - the papers judged him boozer
If their purpose was to shame
There was nothing to be gained
They just added to our pain
Nothing will ever be the same again

Those who would make a mockery of his memory
Humiliation of his final solution - think on
Stay awake for you do not know the hour when the Lord cometh . . .
No mention of His truth - our truth - just their truth
But for grace of God not part of their vocabulary
Nothing will ever be the same again

In Heaven true love is found
His sanctuary is in our hearts and the hearts of his descendants
We pray for him and he for us
No doubt, no fear, His loving spirit is near
Please God nothing will ever be the same again.

*Her son's life ends and his mother can only look on
as he is crucified by a mostly male army of newspaper reporters
and medical and legal structures - just as Mary the Mother of Jesus
could only look on as they crucified her son - has a woman's role and
rights in the system really changed that much since biblical times?*

Catherine Fitzpatrick

WOMEN IN MOTION

Emancipation
Brave women fought this cause for the nation
A vote for each, an equalisation
Equitable voting. Jubilation.

Sacrifice
Women rallied to the cause
Mothers, Grandmas, mine and yours
Taking part in two world wars.

Choice
The 'sixties' brought more freedom still
A world gone mad for good or ill
The contraceptive freedom pill.

Appreciation
Sky is the limit for girls today
Work is hard but no dismay
All they ask is equal pay!

Amy Shelton Goodall

21ST CENTURY WOMAN

A woman in 2003 can be described in many ways
The opportunity exists for her to take up a career that pays.
Civil Rights and education has paved the way for many
Women who can achieve a high status and earn a pretty penny.

No need to remain at home all day feeling rather glum
She goes to college, gets a degree, then beats on her own drum.
The expression 'It's a man's world' is now quite absurd
Woman can have her oyster, and insist on having the last word.

Is man completely lost without a woman around
Woman can cope easily without making a sound.
Today's woman can do anything, has she got it made?
She can be a politician, horse trainer, or even join the fire brigade.

Always there will be women who prefer to do light duties
Manicurists, make-up artists, who turn plain women into beauties.
Suffragettes who were determined to get women the vote
Succeeded in giving women the chance to have their say and gloat.

Yes, woman does see herself as equal, that is equal to man
She likes gorgeous flowers and presents,
And to relax on a sunbed for her tan.
At 65 a man plays bowls, watches cricket and takes life rather gently
Whilst a woman of similar age may be seen driving in her Bentley.

Audrey J Henton

MEN VERSUS WOMEN

Equality for women?
Men just say 'Wants binning,
They take our work, they take our pay,
Why should women have a say?'
But what about the work that women do?
Typing, teaching, cleaning the loo.
Nursing the kids when they are sick
Or knowing when they are playing a trick,
Walking the dog, feeding the cat,
Do men like doing jobs like that?
Telephonist, analyst, programmer, technician,
Designer, hairdresser, gardener, politician.
And yes ladies we should be proud,
We should brag and shout out loud,
Women's equality set a new rule,
So go on dear, *you* take the kids to school!

Susan Ellis

MIDLIFE CHOICE

Through 25 years of nursing,
I've led an active life.
I've also been kept busy,
In my other role as wife.

My skills have come in useful,
Helping people locally.
Life is never ever dull,
When you join a charity.

My career may now be over,
Alas due to poorer health.
We've lived a life in clover,
Thanks to the extra wealth.

No doubt I will be sad,
If from my career I part.
But then I may be glad,
To do things closer to heart.

I may not be as active,
Quite as I used to be.
The alternative is becoming attractive,
To spend my time enjoyably.

So, although we'll have less money,
And I'm no longer in my prime.
Part-time work may be the key,
To gaining some quality time!

J Ramsden

WHY?

Why do I have to do the chores while the boys go out to play?
Why must girls learn cooking skills but boys 'get in the way'?
Why do I have to dust and wash and knit and sew and darn,
While boys go out and lark about or sit around and yarn?
Why are my toys just baking sets and ironing boards and prams,
While boys get footballs, trains and cars and super loader vans?
And why, when I go off to work, am I treated like a jerk,
Where men get twice the salary and women twice the work?
Why are all the bosses men when women do it better?
And why do we always put Dear Sir on every business letter?
And why does being married mean the woman stays at home,
And cooks and cleans and minds the kids while men are free to roam?
Why have I had so little when I wanted so much more,
Why? Because I was born in '32 instead of '84.

Cynthia Glasby

ONLY JOKING... OR AM I?

So,
What do I think of this role in my life?
I do quite enjoy it
No 'trouble or strife'
I can stand my own corner
And do my 'own thing'
I can do as I want
But I wish I could sing!
We ladies fought hard
In our battle with men
I'm happy and proud
I am equal with them
We no longer need them
As much as before
I do things myself
Or ask *her* next door!

Colly

SOLITUDE

Walking in solitude it starts to rain
Thinking about us, was it a mistake?
Lingering memories, all so in vain
Desolate dreaming, prolong the heartache

Not to awaken when last we had cared
A lonely lament surrounds each new sigh
Lost in the ether, emotions once shared
Staring through emptiness, tears cloud my eye

Hopes and desires like a wilting flower
Fade into nothingness, wither and die
Left and forsaken for death to devour
Tied to a broken wing, never to fly

Eternal darkness engulfs all despair
Washed by the raindrops too hard to repair

Chris Hill

AGE 50

Age 50 - What does it mean?
It means I'm the same as I've always been
I'm the same size now as when I was sixteen
I will never be a has been

I'm really into Eminem
I can still wear short skirts with the best of them
My legs are slim and still look good
I could pull a guy half my age if I thought I would

I can party and dance all night
I don't need ecstacy to get as high as a kite
Life is fast and exciting
Life is for living not contemplating

I live loud with heavy metal
Ozzy rules - like him I'll never settle
Live life in the fast lane is my way
I'll never get old and grey

I have no time to consider my future
I refuse to be put out to pasture
So to all those people who think 50 is past it
Think again - I'm still with it

Linda J Ventura

IF ONLY

Oh to be thin, oh to be slim
Because it's a sin to be so round
Flesh it abounds
Piling on pounds
Again - I say
That diet begin!

Elizabeth Hayden-Jones

WHAT WOMEN DO FOR LOVE

It must be the oldest trick in the book
He makes me feel so guilty by giving me *that* look
Or a withering glance from under his brow
Worse by far than a blistering full scale row.
Have I committed murder, been adulterous or run over a cat?
Oh no, if only! My crime is much worse than that
I didn't show enough enthusiasm when he played me his song
He must have read my mind which said it went on far too long.
I thought I'd nodded in all the right places and had a convincing smile
Maybe I had him fooled, if only for a little while
But the strumming and caterwauling tested my acting ability too far
When at the back of my mind I was asking, *why did he ever buy*
that guitar?
Men strum, and they strum and they strum some more
They seek our approval though we find it a chore
The three little words that I would never miss
Are when he holds his beloved guitar and says, 'Listen to this.'
Those three little words are not the ones I long to hear him say
I don't think I'll ever hear *them* by that look he is giving me today
I had better boost his ego and try to put things right
Even if it means listening to his guitar all night.
I do not think I would want to discover
Who was his greatest love, myself or another
What woman can compete with the guitar he holds so dear?
It's not the other 'woman' that causes us to fear.
Women can resort to wishing upon a star
But they know they can't compete with man's love for his guitar
Do men and guitars go together like hand in a glove?
It never ceases to amaze me what women will do for love.

Rita Melia

THE INVISIBLE ME

What is this thing that no one can see?
Attacking so hard to bring us to our knees.
The pain and exhaustion, so hard to describe,
The feeling of great loss that wells up inside.
You do not know, you cannot say,
Just how you'll feel from day to day.

It tears at your body and your mind too,
The feeling of helplessness in all that you do.
How can such a thing destroy us so much?
Relying on others with their tender touch,
To help us get by and see us through
This day to day life is all they can do.

Looking back through the years of exhaustion and pain,
Just wondering when I'll be myself once again.
It's a lonely existence wherever you are,
The friends you once had have retreated afar.
They don't come knocking on your door,
Now you're no use to them anymore.

So what of the future, how long will this last?
I'm sure that this question's been asked in the past,
So being realistic as I know I must be,
I look to each day and the other me.
What I must do now is all I can say,
Is to do what I am able in whatever the day.

Pauline Bowden

I Want To Be A Perfect Mum...

I want to be a perfect mum,
I want a perfect child,
I want to live in a perfect world
That's pure and undefiled,
With dream-like home and lots of friends
And status I require,
And also body that's super trim
That'll never overtire!

> I don't want trouble,
> I don't want strife,
> Just a perfect man
> For a perfect wife -
> But when I look
> Up close to me,
> None of this
> Is reality!

Instead I see a worn out mum,
An exasperating child,
And here I am in a complex world,
Polluted and defiled.
Chaotic house, no time for friends -
Where are the hours required?
So out of shape, unrecognised
Yet long to be admired.

> With lots of guilt
> In all I do,
> Apparent choice
> But is this true?
> 'Cos what's the best
> Decision made?
> The juggling game
> Again is played.

So gone's the dream of perfect mum
Or ever perfect child,
They're fading thoughts of a perfect world
That's pure and undefiled.
There's much I want, and yet I know
Such dreams will never be,
Instead I'll strive the harder path
To find the real me;
To make the best of what I have,
Although it may be small,
And so that when all falls apart
I'll be there standing tall!

Hilary Higton

STOP

What drives us, what gives us the steam?
Is it the money or is it the dream?
Is it the rat race that we have entered in?
Or is it our drive too hard to win?

What makes us have no time to rest?
Is it because we want to be the best?
To prove beyond all reasonable doubt
We are the cream of the crop not a drop out.

What makes the clock hands tick so fast?
Stop for a moment and look at your past
The years like lightning, a flash they speed by
And time sprouts tiny wings and flies

Our lives are busy and full of deadlines
Is this really a good sign?
We're all too busy trying to strive to be on top
We never find the time to sit and stop

To take in the beauty of what we've created
By the time we stop it will be belated
They'll be placing us beneath the ground
There will be nothing to be heard - not a single sound

So let us sit back and press pause for a while
Change our living - change our style
Appreciate the good things that we've achieved
Then in the final hour we won't grieve

Listen to the sound of the wind in the air
And the birds flying around without a care
To the feel of the rain tapping against your skin
It is never too late to stop for a time and begin

Michaela Jayne Fairley

WHO'S SHE?

She thought she'd never achieve her goal
To drag herself from that lonely hole
She thought the streets would consume all of her -
Mind, body and soul.

With every sunrise came obstacles to fear
When the night would fall, so would her tears
Tranquillity left her
Only chaos here

She can't close her eyes - she can't sleep
Memories of nightmares still hers to keep
Self denigrating thoughts and
Apathetic feelings creep

She's on the other side now
She dragged herself out
Her mind is sound
She's standing proud

There is always hope
You can break free
I'm living proof
'Cos *she* is me!

Dizzy D

You Are Not Alone

A whisper, did I hear, within my head?
It's gone, how strange, so quiet it is!
My life it's empty now - and this bed,
There, again that voice - I know it's his!

He left us quickly, after weeks of wracking pain,
'Twas hard to watch him suffer, lose his fight for life,
Those many weeks - there it is again,
Now he's at peace and rest, after all the strife.

It's said their spirit stays within your heart.
A good man he, I loved him,
But Death's Angel came and we did part,
He went alone, to meet the reaper grim.

His voice will comfort me, the words he says
Will give me strength to rearrange my life.
His hand will guide my long and lonely way
And help the one he left behind - his wife.

Pamela Carder

HELP ME!

I'm like a monkey in the zoo
Somebody help me, I don't know what to do
Why me? I ask you
Why do you do the things that you do
When you know damn well it hurts me through and through?

I'm so, so young, can't you see?
Oh, you know what you're doing to me
I smell you, as you enter my bedroom
In you creep, as I begin to weep.

Mum can you hear me, as I cry out your name?
In my head I cry out to you
Please stop this hell, I'm going through
Why doesn't she listen, why doesn't he see
What they are both doing to me?
Help me please, somebody
I'm so angry, yet I'm so weak
I shiver inside, as he kisses my cheek.

All I can do is keep telling myself deep down
Someday I'll be old enough to leave this town
Far away I shall go
I guess I will never stop feeling the pain
Of feeling so low.

Ema Charnock

FEELING THIS WAY

Why do I feel this way?
I have so much to be
grateful for every day

My children are healthy
My house is so fine
But I still feel so cloudy
in my mind

My guilt is strong
because of my unease
But I have always felt
I am here just to please

Run me here
Wash my top
Just nip for my ciggies
from the shop

What about me
don't I matter?
All I hear is the 'get me
fetch me' chatter

Where is the girl
I used to be?
I look in the mirror
and I don't see me.

Amanda Hopley

HIM!

I was curled up like a child
    in the corner of the room,
I didn't care what he did
    as long as it was over soon.
He would kick, shout, swear,
    punch me in the face,
I wish I could get out of here,
    just go and hide any place.
I did it once!
    But it was no good - he still came,
Found and grabbed me by my hair,
    beat me all over again.
The police have been and gone away,
    there's nothing they can do,
It's only a domestic today,
    it will blow over soon.
What a joke! No one cares for me,
    he is just a big bully.
So here I stay, battered and crying,
    he walks around laughing, pretending and lying.
One day it will be over,
    you just wait and see,
Even if I have to kill him,
    at least I will be *free!*

Jackie Sutton

CHEATING

You pig! You've been cheating,
Cheating on me!
I'd never have thought
You'd be so unkind.
I trusted you implicitly.
Just shows you what a fool I've been,
I thought I'd found the perfect partner,
A lover and a friend!
I put my faith in you implicitly.
I trusted your love and your arms about me.
I gave you my heart so willingly.
But now I've woken up to see
That this was a dream,
You're really quite mean.
I've opened my eyes,
Seen through your disguise.
You're caring and sharing
Is geared one way.
You live for the day,
But I have to pay.
So now my friend and lover
I don't think I will bother you
Because you've been cheating on me!

Joan E Blissett

TRAPPED

When did your love turn to hate?
And when did my love turn to fear?
Things became clear far too late.
I tremble each time you come near.
How can I set myself free?
How can I ever escape you?
You threaten me constantly.
You've destroyed a love once so true.
It's crossed my mind to kill you
On a countless number of times.
Revenge is long overdue.
A payment for all of your crimes.
But thoughts cannot be made true
As I know where that path will end.
The courts would put faith in you
And a long time in jail I'd spend.
But what if you did kill me
While caught up in a drunken rage?
How would you enter your plea
To prevent time spent in the cage?
Would I have become a nag
Or a slut with no sense of shame
Of my murder would you brag?
My 'attitude' taking the blame.
Of course we know you'd walk free.
The judge would say you had good cause.
But I and women like me
Want equal treatment from the laws.

Cari Hilaire

JUSTICE

We none of us want justice,
When we sin in any way.
Justice tempered with mercy,
Should be the order of the day.

Men had paid lip service to equality
Especially equality under the law,
But somehow one's gender, race or creed
Counts for a lot behind the courtroom door!

We mostly live with decent people.
Our partners don't treat us like slaves,
And we don't let our tempers overrun
When we are fighting or 'making waves'.

For the few whose reactions are violent,
When they have stood all the hurt they can bear,
The jury should try to stand in their place -
'But for the Grace of God', I'd be there'!

While women have to bear children,
And protect them all against harm,
They're vulnerable in so many ways,
To attack from the 'strong in the arm'.

When they've been beaten and they've forgiven
Not once, but again and again
The bubble's burst and the knife's to hand,
Without thought the tormentor is slain.

I think juries should remember
She has borne this over long years,
And a man with a violet temper,
Cares nothing for his loved one's tears!

Joyce M Jones

WHO'S FOR JUSTICE?

No justice on earth for man or beast
No justice for nations as they bicker and fight
It's the way of evil and all that's bad
Justice and good are well out of sight

The life of the sinner, shines at the helm
Goodwill is cast out, to make way for crime
For the law is an ass, a mocker of man
And our judges are well out of line

So bring back hard labour, also the birch
And let's hear again the sentence of death
For as we stand our laws leave us in the lurch
And they are the only justice we have left

Margaret Gurney

WHAT PRICE THE SISTERHOOD?

Betrayed, and bewildered, one careless moment in time,
Lady crossed the line of reason, now her life's not worth a dime,
It was him, or her, oh why can't they see,
Yet, an eye for an eye is how it must be.
They ripped her apart in that cold witness box,
Her side was no match for that cunning old fox,
He wanted blood with her head on a plate,
So, her pleas for mercy were simply too late.
The scales were balanced, the sword was drawn,
Right through Lady's heart from the day she was born,
Madam justice switched sides to the brotherhood that day,
She abandoned the cause and locked the sisterhood away,
Lady's sins were uncovered, self defence bit the dust,
Her monster may be dead, but conviction's a must,
Shame on you all, rough justice cried,
With a beat of the drum as fair play finally died.

Jan Yule

THE DEMON DRINK

A neckline searching for her navel
Skirt that hugged her tight
With stocking tops both peeping lace
She stepped into the night

Car wheels screeched and swerved
Whilst their wide-eyed drivers stared
But she kept trotting on her high-heels
At them her free spirit glared

A pub loomed up to greet her
With its lights and merry din
Her entrance stopped the drinking
As she calmly walked right in

A drunken fool of thirty
Later whisked her home that night
All fifty years and twenty stone
Next day he saw the light!

Kim Montia

POEM REGARDING BEING A WOMAN

Being a woman can be good
Although she is often misunderstood
Hormones accused for this and that
The blame never lies on his mat
Work and play she has to juggle
Cleaning, cooking and an ear for trouble
It's good however to dress up grand
And to be offered that helping hand
The weaker sex we profess to be
But really we are just craftier than he!

H A Speight

A JOB PLEASE

Please give me a job today
Don't say no and send me away.
I'm over fifty and in my prime
I am active and I've got the time,
I've brought up children, well just one
If I say so myself a job well done,
I'm small, slim and very pert
My mind's not gone, I'm still alert,
I'm really helpful and polite
But I'm not saying I'm always right,
I had to learn how to shop, clean and cook
You don't get all that from a book,
I had to do all the household accounts
Making sure of all the amounts,
Cooking the meals without loads of fat
The right nutrition and all that,
When my child was upset I had to keep calm
Soothe trouble waters with a balm,
So, over fifty for a job I go
Please today don't say no,
The employers always seem to ask
What experience have you for the task,
I think, what have I really got
The answer is I have the lot,
I've loads of experience gained in my life
Just as a mother and a wife,
A chance is all I ask of you
Just to show what I can do,
So please give me a job today
Don't say no and send me away.

Valerie Smallwood

HOUSEWIFE BLUES

Time to get up the clock on the wall chimes
Oh no another time
I pull the duvet over my head
It's too early, the day I dread
Another ten minutes won't cause a delay
But then there's breakfast to be put on the tray

Kettle boiled, tea to be done
Settle down and have one

Now it begins
Mom, I'm working late
As she heads off down the garden gate
Daughter gone, just me at home
Time to do the daily round

Washing and dusting done
Now the mending has begun
Bed to be made
Plan the attack
No one else bothers, that's a fact
Time enough to polish the brass
Then around to cut the grass
101 jobs a housewife does
I wonder why she lacks

Solitary hours all this work
Taxing strength I think I'll shirk
Doorbell rings
I wonder who's that
Open the door
It's Postman Pat

Another chore for me to do
This is the wrong colour, it's blue
Postie can't take it back
Until it's been rewrapped

Rest over, now it's dinner
What shall I cook?
Because I'm only a beginner
Flick through the cookbook
Beans on toast I will give it a look

Daughter home, silence broken
What's for dinner, the words are spoken
Sorry love, it's beans on toast
Perhaps tomorrow you will get a roast

I doubt that she retorts
Why don't you take a cookery course?

D Mason

IF ONLY...

If only we could go back in time
And under the past draw a line
Begin again and start anew
What would we change, what would we do?

Equal rights there would be for many
Voice your opinion, if you have any
Young, old, black and white
Who's to say which one is right?

Equal opportunity!
That's what we want for you and me
So speak up and use your voice
Mankind now has far more choice

If only we would swallow our pride
And put our differences to one side
Take seriously our role
But learn our spirit to control

If only people were more polite
And sometimes willing to forego their right
Could forgive and forget
Give each other more respect

Do unto others as they would do unto you
This rule now is applied by few
Let's work together in harmony
And accept each other's equality

So let us learn from our mistake
A better future let us make
Make sure we put the past behind
And build a future of a different kind.

Penny Pritchard

DEMENTIA

It's ten o'clock, your work is done
And now it's time to head for home.
You've done your work, a busy day
Some things you do to earn your pay.
To be a care assistant, you have to care
Be kind and patient, be aware.
Understanding is another quality
Have a good sense of humour, it works for me.
Dementia is a cruel thing, it hits one in a few,
It could happen to me, it could happen to you.
The memory fails, the body fails too,
They forget how to eat, how to go to the loo,
They forget people's faces, whether daughter or son,
Could be husband or wife, they forget everyone.
With senile dementia there's no war to be won,
The brain cells die slowly, one by one.
You see relatives' faces, you know they can't cope,
They look on so helpless and some live n hope.
Father or Mother, is someone they once knew,
Who reared them, taught them and loved them so true.
People with dementia need care of the best,
Given dignity, kindness, love and rest.
A shoulder to lean on, some kind face to see,
Your hand to support them, a care assistant - that's me!

Stella Copson

A Woman's World

Another day, I'm first to rise
In our house, it's no surprise
I wash and dress then creep downstairs
Breakfast in peace, before the chaos
Polished shoes alongside jackets
Schoolbags with books, juice and crisp packets
I think what next? In my daily routine
Ah yes! I remember, load the washing machine
Familiar clothes fill the laundry bag
Trousers, tops, knickers and bras
Thinking ahead about dinner tonight
What can I cook that everyone likes?
I look in the freezer then get out a dish
A quick decision . . . lemon sole fish
Family are up, fed and watered
Husband, son and two daughters
Six hours to myself, what will I do?
Hoover, dust and clean the loo
Hang out the washing, make the beds
Ten minute tea break, a well-earned rest
Clean the windows, polish the brass
Get out the lawnmower, cut the grass
Tummy rumbles, hungry for food
Stop for lunch, while in the mood
I take in the washing and put it away
I'll maybe iron it later today.
A glance at the clock says it's quarter to three
Time to enjoy a quick cup of tea
Ask myself, *why do I do this each day?*
A woman's world? No Way!

Margaret McGowan

TO AN ABSENT FRIEND

Each and every feature,
I can plainly see,
Thus the mind's eye,
Is faultless you'd agree,
So is the pleasure,
In my memory held,
The image clear,
The loneliness dispelled,
For, if the mind's eye,
Does give such pleasantry,
Those miles between,
Can cause no misery.

Mary Hughes

HER EYES DON'T SPARKLE ANYMORE

She was only fourteen, her eyes hiding their secrets
'What have you been up to? She just sits there subdued
Conscious, yet unconscious, was it drugs, sex, which?
'Doctor's tomorrow young lady, you're going on the pill'
She made no movement, there was no expression
My baby's innocence had been taken away
I went away to my bed, to wait on yesterday
The doctor told me, my decision was wise
But I didn't see such judgement in my daughter's eyes
Who's a perfect mother anyway? There are no books
to show mothers the way
It's all down to guesswork, perhaps some deep rooted
inner knowledge, long dead ancestor planted in my brain
A mother's love becomes endless pain, a tangle of emotions,
never really knowing which way to go
She ended up pregnant anyway, nothing I could do would stop that,
she was only seventeen
I love him she'd bawl, but did she know anything at all, of course not,
alas life has trapped her young innocence into motherhood
and from that day on life is never ever the same.

Ann Hathaway

Moving Home

As you pack up all your pieces and tidy them away,
You empty all your cupboards, remembering yesterday,
You browse through lots of memories of happy times you've had,
You're pleased you're finally moving, but you also feel quite sad.

You built your life together and saw your family grown,
A big house has no use now, you want a smaller home,
But you have one major problem - how will it all fit in?
What to take and which to leave - where will you begin?

With furniture and pictures, and possessions you've amassed,
You're moving to your new house with treasures from your past,
It must be quite exciting, starting out anew,
Planning how you'll have the garden and things you want to do.

So take just one last look around before you close the door,
Its bare and cold and empty, it feels like home no more,
The warmth is in your new place and soon it will be shown,
That boxes full of memories will make your new house home.

Kathleen Elaine Evans

TO ME

You're the blue of
A cloudless sky
You're the lull of
A lullaby
You're the sound
Of a waterfall
A nightingale's call
To me you're like
Blossoms in the spring
You represent everything
Worthwhile and true
That's why I'll always
      Love you

Mary Tickle

WHAT IS LOVE . . . ?

When my grandchildren hold my hand, so proud and glad I feel,
And when they say, 'I'll sit next to you,' when we go out for a meal.
This is love.

To go out in the country to see a newborn lamb,
Or when my daughter rings me to ask me how I am.
This is love.

A nice bouquet of flowers to say a big thank you,
A friendly neighbour who knocks on the door - 'Is there anything
                                                                              I can do?'
This is love.

When I am ill, a husband who takes care of me with ease,
A kiss when I am upset, an eagerness to please.
This is love.

People who work with children, the homeless and the poor,
They give their time unselfishly, their skill, concern and more.
This is love.

Those who visit the elderly, nurses who really care,
A ready smile for everyone, an even temper so rare.
This is love.

June Melbourn

WHAT YOU SEE

What you see is what you get.
Well, that's not really true.
I have a face I keep away,
and it's not for you to view.
It's hidden here, behind my eyes,
transparent in the light.
But this profile wears me down,
as it's not a pretty sight.
I never look in mirrors,
because I see what's really there,
and I think it would frighten you,
if my true face were laid bare.
So this mask I wear is fake.
I made it just for you,
and I'm afraid you'll turn your back
if it ever were see-through.
I'll keep the other, out of sight.
I won't put it on display,
and the scars won't be seen,
when you glance my way.
Then you'll only view the surface.
You won't see what's down below,
and my face will stay beneath,
the one you've come to know.

M M Graham

TO FORGIVE

My love for you it has not altered
The way I feel it has not faltered
Even though you hurt me, and made me want to cry
You made me feel my heart would surely break and die
I gave thought for the hurtful things that you've done
My friend you cannot hide, but you still persist to run
For the anger and bitterness you held inside of you
Will not go away, it's within everything you do
Until you learn forgiveness and let these feelings go
Your cruel intentions towards others is all that you will show
I send loving thoughts always out to you
For I care very deeply about you, and the things that you do
I pray one day that someone will take your pain away
So once more you can live and love again some day
For we all have our crosses, our burdens to bear
What life brings us along is not always fair
But we must pick up the pieces and then we carry on
Drawing on our inner strength to make us strong
Learn by our lessons and move our life along
Otherwise we are trapped and stay in the same place
Only hurt and loneliness engraved upon our face

Elizabeth Leach

WOMAN'S WORK

When did it become mine
that washing on the line?

Who gave it to me
that filthy lavatory?

When did I get to own
that dirt on the phone?

Who said it's a must
that I own the dust?

When was it for the best
that I washed the nets?

Whose were the wishes
that gave me the dishes?

Who says all the grime
must be entirely mine?

Gail Sturgess

A Woman's World

Way, way up in the sky
A white little dove, swiftly did fly
Away, away, far across the sea
Which symbols signs of love, oh so free

Yet, a woman's world needs love and care
A man she can be with, to cherish and care
A woman needs love and affection
A man to show his true compassion

Never to bring life of tears
But joy within, without any fears
A man to whisper in her ear
Those three little words, she longs to hear

A man that can only complete her life
A life without anger, trouble or strife
A man who can hold her tenderly
As she melts in his arms, so affectionately

A man that can steal her nights away
Till the dawn breaks, yet to bring another day
Such love that seems so complete
Giving her gifts, with smiles so sweet

A lifetime together, as they grow old
Till, the heavens open, and the clouds, unfold
Like that white little dove that flew
Way past the sea, when the skies were blue

Jean P McGovern

SOMEBODY'S SWEETHEART

Heralded by rhythmic squeaks of the wheels
Impairments proclaim a life almost spent;
Wrapped in an old rug that partly conceals
Hands once so smooth but now wrinkled and bent.

Hair that was not always fluffy and white,
For rich chestnut curls encircled her face;
Sparkling countenance that shone with delight,
And shining eyes that now stare into space.

For she was once young, she hoped, she desired,
When women were servile, their wants suppressed;
But she walked down the aisle, loved and admired,
Her dreams fulfilled with each babe at her breast.

Years of childbearing have taken their toll,
Of selflessness, fairness, humility,
Of giving love from the depths of her soul,
Heeding her marriage vows dutifully.

Life's tribulations with patience she's borne,
She was somebody's daughter, mother, wife,
Deserving of compassion, never scorn,
Somebody's sweetheart, the love of their life.

Hilary J Cairns

THE SNOW-CAPPED HILL

Do you remember when we took our sledges
To the top of the snow-capped hill?
Our laughing voices, the long slide down
In our hearts, the winter's thrill

Now the ground is covered with fallen snow
How I wish we could again play there
A piercing wind blows over the hill
Alone I stand here and stare

I carry the sledge in the back of my mind
You were a friend like no other
I retrace our steps to the top of the hill
And recall you, my older brother

Joan Magennis

DOWN TO THE SHELTER

The noise of the blast, the whole vibration,
Enough to feel that, civilisation
Was coming to a sudden end.
Standing stiff and still, unable to bend.

Alone I stood on the end of the couch,
I fell on the floor, curled in a crouch.
Waiting, for my father's voice to say,
Come quickly, into the shelter to stay.

He had taken my mother and sister first,
Told me to stay there, didn't expect the burst
Of a bomb coming down so soon.
The siren had just begun its doleful tune.

He gathered me, trembling, in his arms,
My tears and scream he gently calms.
Carries me down to the cellar shelter,
Running across the yard in a helter-skelter.

Fear is something always remembered,
The thought of being forgotten had descended,
In my young mind of six-years-old,
A lonely place, forbidding and cold.

It seemed so long, but could only be moments,
That I was left was for good intents.
Mum was ill and could not walk alone,
I was brave, into a young lady had grown.

I was often the strength in the home I found,
When my father, on duty was not around.
The night of the flares was despairing,
No one was there, to see how we were faring.

Helped dress my mother, find sister's shoes,
Arrived at the shelter, where we heard the news,
Henlow was bombed and father was there,
Mum collapsed with her illness, showed only despair.

Seven months pregnant, at the time very ill,
To get her to the shelter took all my will.
When I think back, at the age of six,
I made a lot of decisions to get out of a fix.

Wars make you grow up, too soon full of care.
Robs you of childhood, you just happen to be there.

Doris Kirby

A Tale Of Two Dogs

I know a little dog so cute,
He can play a tune on the flute.
I found out his bark is mute,
But he's such a little beaut!

I met a dog, an ugly brute,
His looks simply didn't suit.
If I saw him on my route,
I'd kick him with my boot!

If beauty met the brute,
I think it could be a hoot.
But if they were to scoot,
Would the owners shoot?

Rosemary Davies

Forgiving

If rich rewarding harmony is what our lives intend,
We cannot hope to find this unless basically we spend . . .
A part of our lives in understanding fallen brothers,
The need of knowing how to aid and truly help the others.

A genuine desire to make for betterment of man,
The promise of reality our forefathers began,
The weaknesses of ours as our daily lives we live,
The weaknesses of others and the power to forgive.

Pearl M Burdock

FAR AWAY

All day I cry, all night I sob
My heart aches, and doesn't throb
Everything's messed up
And I can't clear my mind
Of images of you
And another love you'll find
My heart is broken
And can barely beat
10 days to go
Until we next meet
I hate hearing your voice
So far away
But there was nothing I could do
To make you stay
I bet you're so happy
Laying in the sun
But here it's raining
And for my heart it's no fun
I can't wait till the day
I next see your face
To feel your kiss
And your warm embrace

Sophie Long

JUDGE ME NOT

Sift through the dirt and what do you see?
A soul too ugly to be free
Living life with sweat and pain
Hoping and wishing to go insane.

I am not your saviour, send me away
I cannot but another minute pay
The debt I owe is more than my life's own
Into the lions' den I'd wish to be thrown.

Cut me, bite me, pain is my solace
Comfort only in what I hate
See my pain, embrace my blood
Let it flow in a blessed flood.

Let me take another life into my death
For I'd give my life to see his last breath
Blood for blood, pain for pain
Release this poison from my vein.

Donna-Marie Capper

I Still Love You

We met across a crowded room
Yet the area was so small
I couldn't see your face
But I knew you stood tall
The way you spoke reminded me
Of a gentle, warming breeze
I always shuddered deep inside
Because of the way you teased
And yet within my heart I knew
We would get together
I thought our love was strong enough
And would always last forever
But here I sit, alone at night
And wonder where you are
I wish I could reach out to you
But you are so far
With these words unspoken
I hope you read one day
My words will come across to you
As they reach out and say
I still love you

Shahdaroba

THE WEDDING DAY

At last the day is here, the happiest of your life,
The day you stop being single and become young Brian's wife.
And as I watch you say your vows I know I'll shed some tears,
As memories crowd into my heart of all those foregone years.
I held you as a baby, tenderly in my arms,
As a toddler you sat upon my knee, dazzling with your charms.
I watched you grow from coltish girl into a woman fine,
And I was glad, so very glad, that I could say 'she's mine'.
I've watched you meet your disappointments with a strength
                                                beyond your years,
I've seen you deal with pain, with laughter not with tears.
I've watched you confront adversity and take it on the chin,
Square your shoulders, stand up tall, and begin your life again.
And through it all I've loved you, although sometimes silently,
And been so proud and grateful that you were born to me.
And as you start your new life with your own special boy,
I wish you love and happiness, prosperity and joy.

Pamela Matthews

LOVE WILL COME

Don't ever stop searching
For a love strong and true
He is in this world somewhere
And he is searching for you.

Perhaps you have met him
You could even be friends
That's how it all starts
Who knows where it ends.

Who knows if you've passed him
In some crowded street
Just one fleeting glance
And your heart skips a beat.

Then later, a meeting
Was it only by chance?
But no, cupid was working
On two lives to enhance.

So he arranged for the union
Of two lonely hearts
And a bright, happy future
For them will now start!

Paula M R Jackson

A SINGLE FLOWER

When I'm here and all alone,
And you my love are safe at home,

I long to see you once again,
When your kisses will relieve the pain,

Relieve the pain within my heart,
Which I have to bear whilst we're apart,

For I only live each day to see,
My lover whose become for me,

The reason why I want to live,
The reason why I want to give,

A token life a single flower,
A simple thing to show the power,

Of love which always will emerge,
And with its magic swift submerge.

All the heartache form the past,
And bring a joy ordained to last.

John Terry

TO BE ALONE

I'm scared of being lonely
I'm scared of being poor
Of never seeing anyone
No knock upon the door.

I'm scared of being lonely
With no one else to share
No food or heat, no one to meet
No one else to care.

I'm scared of being lonely
My life has passed me by
My love has failed, my children gone
The clock's stopped telling time.

I'm scared of being lonely
Where did it all go wrong?
I always thought I gave so much
But now my life's just gone.

I'm scared of being lonely
I sit and wonder why
And then the day just closes
And the tears just fill my eyes.

S Stark

BROKEN HEART

I will love you
Wherever you are
In my dreams
I see your smiling face
And hear the sound
Of your laughter
Ringing all around
It's so sad
We had to part
But it was you
That wanted to be free
So you could love
Someone other than me
I will never love again
As things would
Never be the same
Especially when
I hear your name
For you will
Always have a place
Within my heart

Joyce Sherwood

FORBIDDEN LOVE

It feels so good between you and I
This love of secrecy
This love of guilt
It feels so good, there is no way out
Love gets stronger without a doubt.

Forbidden love is a cruel fate
You fall in love when it's far too late
Love I assume will conquer all
This love that we share will never fall.

People say it will never last
Broken hearts, sadness and tears
It's one of my greatest fears
But with love like this, which seems so strong,
Surely this love is not so wrong?

Jennifer Jackson

REFLECTING ON THE PAST

A figure framed in the window,
a vision encircled in light
recalls to mind
some happier time:
an evocative sight.

But reflections were casting more shadows
though light from the window was seen,
'til a darkening gloom
pervaded the room
where love had been.

The reflections transformed to mere shadows
and reality changed to a dream;
leaving no trace,
just an empty space,
where you had been.

Susan Turner

MY LOVE'S CHERISHED MEMORY

Farewell my dear and precious love
Wherever now you may be
I have not one regret
For all the love that came from me

You gave me the chance to love again
And allowed me to open that door
So much love did I feel for you
Nobody could of loved you more

You went away and how I cried
My heart was torn apart
But you will always have a special place
Here deep within my heart

I will remember those happy times
The many hours we shared together
Yes, I will smile as I think of you
Cherished memories I will have forever

The physical presence can be removed
Then is such pain one has to suffer
But with you I learned I can love again
And how much love I have to offer

So I thank you now for all that we had
For all that I am now aware
You showed me how much love I have
And how much I can truly care

So now as I go forward in life
On this pathway in front of me
Your footsteps will remain in my heart
My love's cherished memory.

Christine Cyster

THE PATH OF LOVE

The one who gives a lot in love also expects a lot,
But not before tears are shed and emotions run high.
Thus leaving you exposed and in a vulnerable state.
It is said that the path of true love never did run smoothly.

Ise Obomhense

LOVE'S PIT

Entering the chasm of regret,
I set my heart upon
The stairwell of the king
Where tears sing
The sorrows of antiquity.

From far below
The claws of Christ
Rip open this lost wound,
Cleansing blood from deeps
Where Eros once had been asleep.

I'm in the pit!
Dug deeper from my fateful plunge -
The loss of father, lover, son -
And weeping unrelentingly,
The gods wring
The sponge of this dark destiny
(Imprinted by the centuries)
Of falling through the planets' gates
To Earth to birth to fate.

My soul fit his soul like a glove
Delirious projection
Primordial rejection;
Millennia of unrequited love.

Seven years, another round is done;
I stay inside my soggy grief
Awaiting Grace
To come with her relief.

'You entered through love's ravishment
Then found the poisoned kiss
You're knitted now, you're single, one;
I am the eyes of Artemis.'

Pamela Preston

NEW VALENTINE

Although I have not known you long, this Valentine I send,
Hoping this will develop into more than just a friend,
And as the months go passing by, a love will surely grow,
For I am wishing with this card, this feeling you will know.

A flame that's slowly kindling, a warm from deep within,
A longing fro the days to pass, till we will meet again,
And hopefully as this year ends, these thoughts at last will show,
This Valentine I send to you, has made those feelings grow.

So to my newfound Valentine, I wish you deep felt love,
And ask the guardian angel, who cares for you above,
To send his arrow to your heart, to light the waiting flame,
Then I can tell you by next year, from whence this message came.

K Townsley

NOT ALONE

Sitting alone in my fireside chair
I gaze across and remember you there
Wallowing in all of my fond memories
Of togetherness, happiness and even the tears.

Listening to music that we so enjoyed
Mutual friends who now we avoid
Not knowing what to say, or even mention your name
My house empty now, where once friends came

But I use your name each and every day
When I pass your photograph, or touch your chair
I'm not alone, or bitter, I have no fear
I know when I need you, you'll always be there.

Morag Kilpatrick

DEAR JACK

No plans this year to go away
Not even for a half a day
Important things we have to face
Scary things that take first place
To any other wants or needs
This fact is where we both agreed
When April comes you have to go
For treatment on this painful growth
That's caused you such a lot of pain
I pray they'll make you well again
And that your heart that isn't strong
Will bear the trauma all along
We know it's going to take some time
'Fore Dryfields Hill again you'll climb
But loving thoughts and nursing care
Will ascertain that you get there
Be brave dear man, you'll see it through
My loving thoughts are there with you
My hopes and prayers were all in vain
My dear man I'll not see again
Until we meet at Heaven's gate
How long I wonder will I wait

Joan Fletcher

As Times Go By

Playing in the sun,
Having fun with make-believe.
My mother comes to the door,
I have to do my maths for primary four.

Walking with my friends,
Gossip and laughter flow.
The school disco will soon be here,
It's summertime in second year.

Sitting in my room,
In my purpose made alienation.
I'm a Goth and that's my parents' fear,
I'm growing up and in fourth year.

Enjoying the free times after moving out,
It's constant parties with my friends.
Why not have a good time?
It's the summer of 1999.

Unsteady times and all the rest,
My head said no, my heart said yes.
Our loss cost us each other's fun,
In the summer of 2001.

Relaxing on the sofa,
Admiring this month's pay slip.
I'll buy all the things I want,
And things to do for you and me.
Why not, it's almost summer 2003.

Carrie Stuart

LOSING YOU

Last spring came and went so fast
I never saw the sun,
That was the time I lost you,
My new life had begun.

I walked with heavy heart then,
I never saw the snowdrops grow
Or the blossom on the trees,
Why did you have to go?

I've always watched the spring unfold,
New leaves would then appear,
But last spring I saw it all,
Through many falling tears.

Diane Stead

MISSING YOU

M aybe it was your time to go
I still imagine you are here
S ometimes I think I see you
S ometimes, I feel you near
I wonder what you're doing
N ow you're up there high above
G randpa Joe, I hope has found you

Y ou can give him all my love
O ne day we'll no longer be apart
U ntil then I'll hold you in my heart

J Preston

SOUL JOURNEY

Beautiful are memories
of a moonlit night with you,
The spark of love rekindled
when all the world was new.

My heart told me I'd known you
in times so long ago,
For something deep inside
had set my soul aglow.

As I looked into your eyes
I knew you felt it too,
The longing grew between us
just like it used to do.

You took my hand in yours
I felt a burning flame,
Such a familiar feeling
I knew from whence it came.

Inside my spirit soared
to heights that once we knew,
And through the mists of time
I recalled my love for you.

Soul mates reunited
bound by the ties of past,
Through each and every age
this perfect love would last.

So at our journey's end
when the time has come to part,
Somewhere a silver cord
will link us heart to heart.

Marian Jones

FOREVER

With my heart heavy
and my soul sad
I say goodbye to that lovely lad
I reach over to dry his tears
'Promise me you won't wait for years'
he looked at me through his sorrowful eyes
and in silent he said his goodbyes
'I promise I won't wait for years'
he whispered as we parted hands
the sea washing away
our footprints in the sand.

Emma Scott

SUBMISSIONS INVITED
SOMETHING FOR EVERYONE

WOMENSWORDS 2003 - Strictly women, have your say the female way!

POETRY NOW 2003 - Any subject, any style, any time.

STRONGWORDS 2003 - Warning! Opinionated and have strong views. (Not for the faint-hearted)

All poems no longer than 30 lines.
Always welcome! No fee!
Cash Prizes to be won!

Mark your envelope (eg Poetry Now) *2003*
Send to: Forward Press Ltd
Remus House, Coltsfoot Drive,
Peterborough, PE2 9JX

OVER £10,000 POETRY PRIZES TO BE WON!
Judging will take place in October 2003